LIVING *through* HISTORY

Foundation Edition

Black Peoples
of the Americas

Fiona Reynoldson
and
David Taylor

Heinemann

Heinemann Library, Halley Court,
Jordan Hill, Oxford OX2 8EJ
a division of Reed Educational and Professional
Publishing Ltd

OXFORD MELBOURNE AUCKLAND
JOHANNESBURG BLANTYRE GABORONE
IBADAN PORTSMOUTH (NH) USA CHICAGO

Heinemann is a registered trademark of
Reed Educational and Professional
Publishing Ltd.

First published 1998

09 08 07 06 05 04 03 02 01
10 9 8 7 6 5

British Library cataloguing in Publication data
for this title is available from the British Library.

ISBN 0 435 30990 0

Designed and produced by Dennis Fairey
and Associates Ltd.

Illustrated by Sally Artz, John James,
Sally Launder, Arthur Phillips, Keith Richmond
and Stephen Wisdom.

Photographic acknowledgements

The authors and publisher would like to
thank the following for permission to
reproduce photographs:

Cover photo: Popperfoto

Ancient Art & Architecture Collection/
Ronald Sheridan: 2.1B
Associated Press: 5.6A p.51
Associated Press/Topham: 6.2C
Ida Berman, New York: 5.8B
BFI Stills: 5.2D
Bridgeman Art Library: 2.3A, 3.4B
British Museum: 2.2A
Chicago Historical Society: 3.5A, 5.5A
Corbis-Bettmann: p. 29, 4.1B, 4.3B, 5.1A, 5.2B,
5.3A

Corbis-Bettmann/UPI: 3.4E, 5.1C, 5.2C, 5.3D,
p. 52, 6.2B
Corcoran Gallery of Art, Washington DC: 4.4B
Denver Public Library: p. 8
Mary Evans Picture Library: 2.2C
The Granger Collection, New York: 4.3C
Kansas Collection, University of Kansas: p. 7
Library of Congress, Washington DC: 5.4C
Magnum Photos/Bruce Davidson: 6.1C
Magnum Photos/Danny Lyon: 5.8C
Menil Collection, Houston: 2.4B
Nebraska State Historical Society: p. 9
Peter Newark's Pictures: 1.2B, C, 3.6A, 4.2B
New Haven Colony Historical Society: 3.4D
New York Historical Society: 4.2A
Nickelodeon Television: 6.3B
Popperfoto: 5.4A
Popperfoto/Reuters/Fabrizio Bensch: p.60
Charmian Reading, New York: 6.1D
Roger-Viollet: 3.4C
Schomburg Center for Research in Black Culture,
New York: 2.3B, 3.2A, 4.4A
Worldwide Photos/Birmingham Public
Library/Birmingham News, Alabama: 5.7B

The publishers have made evey effort to trace
copyright holders of material in this book.
Any omissions will be rectified in subsequent
printings if notice is given to the publisher.

Printed in Spain by Edelvives

CONTENTS

What this book is about

This book is about the history of black people in America and the West Indies.

Most black people were taken to America and the West Indies as **slaves**.

Ships full of slaves crossed the Atlantic Ocean. It was a long and very rough journey (look at the map).

Words

Slave: A slave was owned by a master. The slave had to work for the master.

Plantation: A farm that grows cotton, sugar or tobacco.

Most black people came to America from Africa as slaves. This map shows the journey of the slave ships.

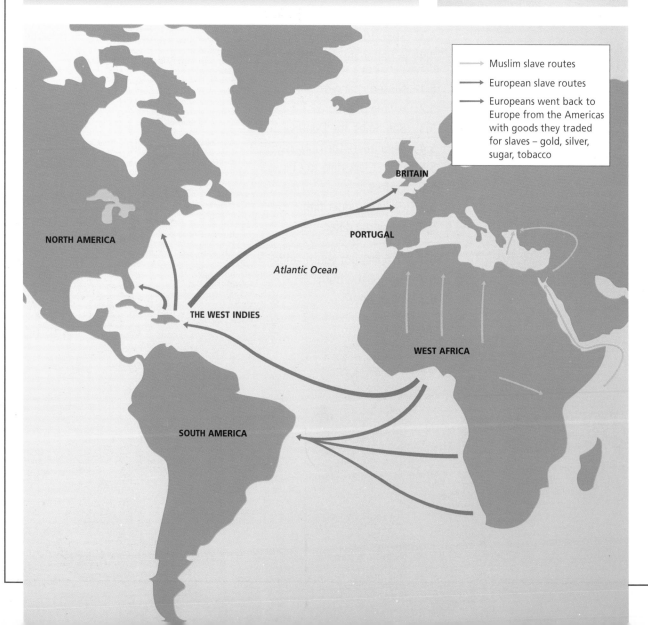

Muslim slave routes

European slave routes

Europeans went back to Europe from the Americas with goods they traded for slaves – gold, silver, sugar, tobacco

BRITAIN

NORTH AMERICA

PORTUGAL

Atlantic Ocean

THE WEST INDIES

WEST AFRICA

SOUTH AMERICA

Hard work and no freedom

Black people from Africa were sold to be slaves in America. They were made to work on **plantations**.

The work was hard. Often the slaves were very badly treated by their masters. Slaves did not have any freedom.

Worse treatment than white people

Slavery was stopped in America in 1865. Black slaves became free people.

Black people thought that they would now have the same rights as white people. They thought they would be equal with white people.

But this did not happen. Black people in America were still badly treated. Often people would not give them jobs just because they were black.

This book is the story of how black Americans have fought to be free and equal. Read on!

Source A

Black slaves working on a plantation in the early 1800s.

What is prejudice?

Prejudice is thinking badly about someone or something, without having a reason to.

The white people in the picture are being prejudiced.

Why white people treated black people badly.

They are not as clever as whites. They need telling what to do, like children.

They are lazy. Without us, they sit around all day.

They are dangerous. Give them half a chance and they will rob you, or worse.

We're just ordinary people. Give us a chance.

Black people left out

The story of the American Wild West has been told mainly by white story-tellers and film-makers. They tell how the 'good' white cowboys fought the 'bad' Indians.

Black people have been left out of the story on purpose. We are left thinking that there were no black people in the West.

Lots of black people

The truth is the opposite! There were lots of black people in the West of America.

There were black cowboys, black farmers, black slaves, black criminals and black miners. Here are the stories of some of them.

Source A

A black American said this in 1926.

If black people are left out of history books, it looks like they are not important.

This map shows the western states of America.

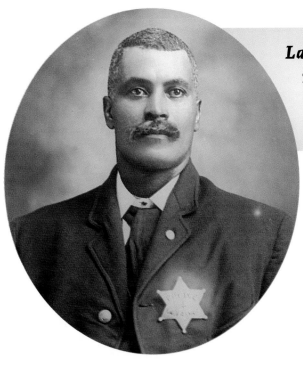

Law and order

Some towns had black sheriffs. This man was the sheriff of Abilene, a cattle town in the West. The sheriff kept law and order.

Source B

Black and white miners, digging for gold.

ALVIN COFFEY

Alvin Coffey was a black slave in America.

In 1849 his master took him west to California.

They went to look for gold. A lot of other people went too. It was called the Californian Gold Rush.

Alvin and his master had a long, hard journey to get to California.

When they reached California, they built a log cabin to live in.

They dug for gold. Alvin made $5,000 for his master and $700 for himself.

He was going to buy his freedom, but his master stole his savings.

Alvin had to start saving again. In the end, he saved enough money to buy his freedom.

Black cowboys

Black cowboys were paid the same as white cowboys.

Nat Love was a famous black cowboy. He wrote his life-story.

He said he was treated as an equal by the white cowboys.

When he gave up being a cowboy, he went to work on the railways.

20,000 white cowboys   10,000 black cowboys

The number of black and white cowboys in the West.

Black cowboys were very good at riding and lassooing cattle.

ISOM DART

Some black people in the West broke the law a lot.

Isom Dart was born a slave in 1849.

In 1865 he moved to the West.

He became a cattle thief.

In 1900 Dart was shot dead.

Questions

1 Read **Black people left out** on page 6.

   Why do we not see many black people in films or books about the Wild West?

2 Read about **Alvin Coffey** on page 7.

   Explain how Alvin Coffey got his freedom.

3 Read **Black cowboys** on page 8.

   a How many black cowboys were there?
   b How were black cowboys treated?

4 Look back over pages 8–9. Name a black cattle thief and a kind black woman who lived in the West.

Black women in the West

Black women went west with their families or masters. They sometimes ended up going their own way.

BIDDY MASON

Biddy was a slave. In 1849 she was taken to California by her master. He was looking for gold.

Biddy's master went home after a while. But Biddy and her three daughters stayed. Biddy made some money and bought some land.

Biddy was kind. She gave money away for building schools and churches. She also helped the poor.

Black settlers

When they got their freedom, some black slave families moved to the West. The picture below shows a black family who went to live in the West. Their house is made out of turf. They have two buggies and a wind pump to pump water up from the ground.

MARY FIELDS

Mary was born a slave in the 1830s.

She moved West when she was about fifty years old.

She was a tough woman and had lots of jobs. When she was sixty, she was a stage coach driver! Then she ran a laundry.

One day she was in the saloon. A man did not pay for his drink, so Mary chased him and knocked him out!

Mary died in 1914.

The history of West Africa

Hundreds of years ago, West Africa was split into kingdoms.

There were lots of different **tribes** (groups) of black people.

Craftspeople

The black people of West Africa were clever. They had the skill to make beautiful things out of gold, silver and brass (see Source A and Source B).

Source A

A description of the King of Ghana in 1107.

He has over 200,000 warriors and is very rich.

He is guarded by ten men with gold-handled swords.

Even his dogs have collars made out of gold and silver.

Some early West African kingdoms

Nok	Ife
Ghana	Benin
Mali	Songhai

Some kingdoms and tribes of West Africa in about 1400.

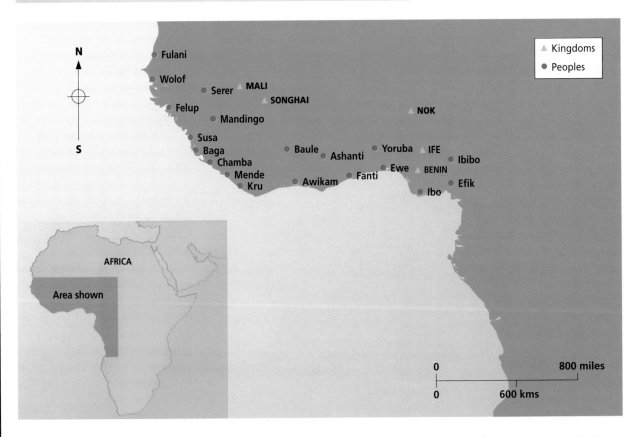

10

War between kingdoms

The black kingdoms often fought each other. Warriors took prisoners after a battle.

The prisoners were kept as slaves.

Trade with the Arabs

The Arabs lived in North Africa.

They went to West Africa and took salt, spices and books. Then they returned home with gold and slaves.

The Arabs were **Muslims**.

They worshipped Allah. Some black West Africans also became Muslims.

A head made out of brass. It was made in the kingdom of Ife. The people of West Africa were very good at sculptures like this.

Slavery in Africa before white people arrived

White people first arrived in Africa in the 1440s.

There was slavery in Africa before white people came. But it was different from the slavery that came later.

1 Most slaves were captured in battles. Slaves worked for the people who captured them.

2 In some kingdoms, people were made slaves if they broke the law.

3 Some slaves were sold to the Arabs. The Arabs were kind to their slaves.

Questions

1 Read Source A.

What does the source tell us about this king?

2 Look at Source B.

What does the source tell us about the black people of Africa?

White people arrive in West Africa

In the 1440s, white sailors from Portugal reached West Africa. They captured black people and took them back to Portugal to be slaves.

Spain, Portugal and America

In the 1490s, sailors from Spain and Portugal landed in America and the West Indies. Settlers from Spain and Portugal went to live there.

The land was empty and wild. There was lots of work to be done. Houses had to be built and farms started. At first, the settlers used white workers from Europe.

Sugar and tobacco

The settlers started to grow sugar and tobacco. Their farms grew bigger, so they needed more workers. They decided to bring black slaves from Africa to work on their farms.

Source A

The diagram below shows how black African people ended up in America.

White settlers went to America.

They grew sugar and tobacco.

There were not enough white workers.

Black slaves were brought from Africa.

A model of a white soldier from Europe. It was made out of bronze by a black African.

Questions

1 Read page 12.

    a When did white people from Spain and Portugal first go to America?

    b Why did they need lots of workers?

    c What did they do to get more workers?

2 Read **England joins in** on page 13.

    Why did lots of English captains start trading in black slaves?

England joins in

In the 1500s, English ships started to take black Africans to America.

Captains realised that there was a lot of money to be made by selling black slaves.

The first English captain to sell black slaves was Sir John Hawkins in 1562.

The slave trade grows

By the late 1700s, many other captains had started dealing in slaves.

In 1771 alone, 92 English ships took nearly 50,000 slaves from Africa to America.

Slavery after 1440

Slavery changed after 1440 when white people got involved.

1 Trading in slaves became a big business. Lots of money was made.

2 Trading in slaves became an overseas trade. It was a long way from Africa to America. Once in America, a black slave would not be able to get back.

3 The treatment of black slaves became very cruel.

Source B

Hans Staden tells how the Spanish treated black slaves. Staden was from Holland. He visited Brazil in the 1540s.

Some Spanish masters are very cruel to their slaves.

They torture the slaves for doing the slightest thing wrong.

Some slaves have run away. When I was in Brazil, I saw slaves rebelling.

A drawing from a book by Hans Staden. It shows slaves being beaten.

Source C

Big business

By the 1700s, the slave trade was big business. Thousands of black slaves were taken from Africa to America. One of them was Olaudah Equiano.

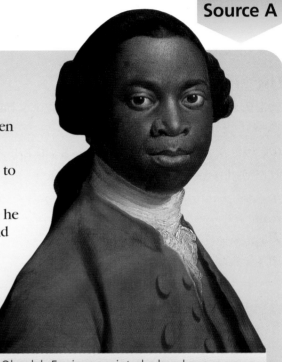

Source A

OLAUDAH EQUIANO

Olaudah was born in West Africa in 1745.

In 1755 he was kidnapped by black people and taken to the coast.

Olaudah was put on a slave ship. He was taken first to the West Indies, then to America.

Between 1756 and 1766 Olaudah was a slave. Then he bought his freedom for £40. He went to England and got married.

In 1777 he started to make speeches in England, saying that slavery was cruel and should be stopped.

In 1789 he wrote his life-story. Many people read it. Olaudah died in 1797.

Olaudah Equiano, painted when he was a free man.

Olaudah's life-story

Here is part of Olaudah's story.

1 Capture

One day my parents were out. I was alone in the house with my sister.

Two men and a woman got into the house and took us away. I called for help, but I was put into a sack. I could not escape. I was taken to the coast. There was a ship waiting to take slaves to the West Indies.

2 On board the ship

The ship's crew had white skin. I had not seen a white person before. The crew pushed me about. I thought they were going to eat me.

There were many other black people on board. They were chained together.

I was so scared that I fainted.

3 Crossing the sea

I was put under the deck. The smell was awful.

People were crying. I was flogged because I would not eat my food.

I did not feel like eating.

I was told that I would be sold to white people in America as a slave.

The smell and heat below the deck got worse. We had to use big tubs to go to the toilet. There was sickness and a lot of black people died.

It was a horrifying journey. I spent some of the time on the top deck. They said I was too young to be in chains. I was lucky.

Source B

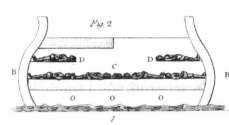

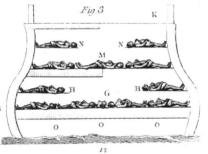

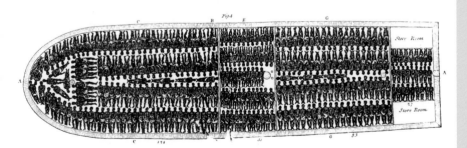

How a slave ship was loaded with slaves. The slaves were packed in very close together. It was very cruel. Conditions were so bad that many slaves died on the journey. The bodies were thrown overboard.

Questions

1 Read the box on page 14. Write down these events in the correct order.

- Olaudah made speeches saying slavery was cruel.
- Olaudah was kidnapped from his village in Africa.
- Olaudah worked as a slave.
- Olaudah wrote his life-story.
- Olaudah bought his freedom.
- Olaudah was taken to America.

2 Can you think why Olaudah Equiano might have thought the white people would eat him?

2.4 WHAT HAPPENED ON ARRIVAL?

On arrival the slaves were split up from their family and friends. They were sold to merchants and planters (see Source A).

Once sold, slaves became the property of their master. They had to do as they were told.

Source A

Olaudah Equiano tells of his arrival in the West Indies.

When we arrived, merchants and planters came on to the ship.

They made us jump about to see if we were fit.

The next day we were sold. The buyers rushed to get the slaves they wanted.

Families and friends were split up. They never saw each other again.

What's your name?

Slaves could not keep their own name. They were given a new name when they reached the West Indies. Then, when they were sold, their master often changed their name again. Olaudah Equiano was first called Michael, then Jacob, then Gustavus.

A slave being whipped for breaking the rules. The picture was painted in 1849.

Source B

From person to possession

1

Families and friends split up.

2

Slaves sold.

3

Your name is 'James Jones'.

Slaves named by owner.

4

This is James, Anthony. Make him work hard.

Yes, master Jones.

Slaves set against each other by putting some in charge of the rest.

5

No talking or singing! No meetings after work!

Slaves stopped from getting together in groups.

6

I've sold you, James. You are 'James Smith' now.

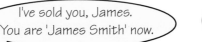

Slave families broken up more than once.

7 Slaves not allowed to read and write or worship as they want.

Cruel punishments for breaking the rules or running away.

Questions

Read page 16.

1 Who bought the slaves?

2 What happened to families?

3 What happened to the slaves' names?

4 What happened if a slave broke the rules?

3.1 THE WAR OF INDEPENDENCE

What was the war about?

Britain ruled thirteen colonies in America.

By 1776 the colonies had grown tired of British rule. They did not like having to pay taxes to Britain.

The colonies wanted to be **independent** and run their own government.

The colonies started a war against Britain to get their independence.

Source B

A black person said this to the American government in 1791.

You say everyone is equal. Then why do you keep so many black people in slavery?

Source A

From the American Declaration of Independence, 4 July 1776.

All men are equal. God gave all men life, freedom and the right to be happy.

Black people and the war

Some free black people fought against the British.

Some black slaves fought for the British.

The slaves thought they would get their freedom if Britain won the war.

But in 1783 Britain gave up the fight. America was free of Britain.

What would happen to black slaves now?

Source C

A newspaper report of the funeral of men killed fighting against the British in 1770.

Last Thursday, the bodies of Samuel Grey, Samuel Maverick, James Caldwell and Crispus Atticus were buried.

They were killed in the bloody massacre last Monday.

Most of the shops in town were shut and all the bells were rung.

Lots of people came to watch. Everyone was terribly upset.

CRISPUS ATTICUS

In 1770 there was a riot in Boston against the British.

Four Americans were shot dead by British soldiers. It was called the Boston Massacre. One of the men shot was Crispus Atticus. He was a black slave who had run away from his master.

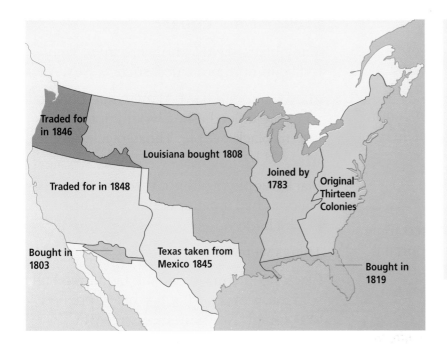

This map shows how the United States grew.

The country was divided into states.

Each state could decide whether to allow slavery or not.

Map labels:
- Traded for in 1846
- Louisiana bought 1808
- Joined by 1783
- Original Thirteen Colonies
- Traded for in 1848
- Bought in 1803
- Texas taken from Mexico 1845
- Bought in 1819

The United States of America

After the war, the thirteen colonies became states. Together they made up the United States of America (USA). Later on, more states joined the USA.

Freedom for slaves?

A **constitution** (list of rules) was written to say how the USA should be run.

The American government had said that all men were equal (see Source A). So black slaves hoped to be set free.

But the new rules said that states could keep slaves if they wanted to.

The southern states grew cotton. Lots of people wanted cotton.

Farmers in the South said it was impossible to grow enough cotton without using slaves. So they kept their slaves.

Source D

The number of slaves in the southern states.

1800	1,000,000
1820	1,500,000
1840	2,500,000
1860	4,000,000

Questions

Read **Freedom for slaves?** and look at Source D.

1 Why did black slaves hope to be freed after the War of Independence?

2 Why did the number of slaves go up in the southern states?

The South needed slaves

There was a big demand for cotton. It was taking over from wool as the main type of cloth.

Machines were invented to spin cotton more quickly. Plantation owners in the South said they could not do without slaves.

The North frees slaves

The northern states grew tobacco. But tobacco was becoming less important. So tobacco growers did not need as many slaves.

They let a lot of slaves go free.

Free but not equal

Many black slaves who were freed went to live in northern cities, such as New York.

They found life hard. Many white people were prejudiced. They would not give jobs to black people. Those black people who did have jobs were badly paid.

Black people could not vote. White children had a better education than black children.

Things were far from equal.

Black people might also be kidnapped and sold into slavery. That is what happened to Solomon Northrup (see page 21).

The map shows which states still had slaves in 1860. Are they in the North or the South?

Slave states in 1860

Free states in 1860

Boundary between free and slave states

CANADA

Oregon

American Territories not divided into states yet

California

Kansas

Minnesota

Wisconsin

Iowa

Illinois

Michigan

Indiana

Ohio

Missouri

Kentucky

Tennessee

Arkansas

Mississippi

Louisiana

Alabama

Georgia

Texas

MEXICO

Vermont

Maine

Massachusetts

New York

New Hampshire

Rhode Island

Connecticut

New Jersey

Pennsylvania

Maryland

Virginia

North Carolina

South Carolina

THE STORY OF SOLOMON NORTHRUP

Solomon was a black person. He was born in New York in 1808.

Solomon's father was a freed slave. He was happy with his wife and children.

Solomon played the violin. One day in 1841, two white men offered him a job in their circus. Solomon took it because the pay was good.

The circus reached Washington. Solomon was having a drink with the two men. They drugged Solomon's drink.

When Solomon woke up, he was chained up and alone in the dark.

Solomon realised he had been kidnapped. The white men beat him up.

Then Solomon was taken to New Orleans and sold into slavery. He was a slave for the next twelve years.

In the end, a lawyer helped him to get his freedom. But he died soon afterwards.

The price of a slave

Slaves varied in price. The price depended on how healthy the slave was, and how badly he or she was needed.

Here are the prices paid by one owner for young male slaves in different years:

1800	$70
1840	$600
1850	$1,500
1860	$2,000

Source A

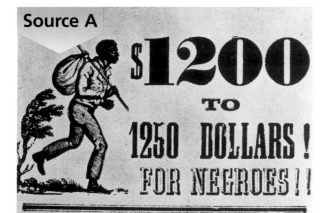

$1200 TO 1250 DOLLARS! FOR NEGROES!!

THE undersigned wishes to purchase a large lot of NEGROES for the New Orleans market. I will pay $1200 to $1250 for No. 1 young men, and $850 to $1000 for No. 1 young women. In fact I will pay more for likely

NEGROES,

Than any other trader in Kentucky. My office is adjoining the Broadway Hotel, on Broadway, Lexington, Ky., where I or my Agent can always be found.

WM. F. TALBOTT.

LEXINGTON, JULY 2, 1853.

Questions

1 Look at the map on page 20. Name three states that still had slavery in 1860.

2 Read **The North frees slaves**.

   Why did the northern states free slaves?

3 Read **Free but not equal**.

   Write down two things to show that black people were not treated as equal to white people.

Slaves were in demand in the South. This is an advert for slaves. 'Negro' was the word used for a black person. People don't use it these days because they think it is very insulting.

3.3 SHOULD SLAVERY BE ABOLISHED?

Slaves must be set free

Many people, black and white, said it was wrong to keep slaves. They started to argue that slaves should be set free.

People who wanted slaves to be set free were called **abolitionists**.

Leaflets and speeches

The abolitionists printed leaflets and made speeches.

They also printed a newspaper called the *Liberator*. It was full of stories about black slaves being cruelly treated. Many white people were shocked.

Sojourner Truth (1797–1883)

Sojourner was a black slave, but she ran away from her master.

She was an abolitionist. She went round making speeches about getting slavery banned. She was very famous.

In 1986 the American government issued a stamp with Sojourner on it. This was to remember all she did to get slaves freed.

Slavery is wrong. Black people are just like anyone else. They should have equal chances.

What a silly idea! They should be free; but they are not equal. They are like simple children.

Free them and send them back home to Africa. They belong there. Staying here will cause problems.

Free them and train them to work for us. They will be loyal and hard-working and grateful. But they need to be told what to do.

Free us, give us a chance of equal education and jobs, then you will see what we can do.

Abolitionists had different views.

What was said against slavery

Source A

An American preacher said this in 1839.

- Slavery is a curse.

- Slaves are treated like animals.

- Slaves are worked too hard.

- They do not get enough rest.

- Slaves are not well fed.

- They are made to live in bad houses.

- Slaves are made to wear chains and iron collars with prongs.

- Slaves are beaten and then have salt rubbed into the cuts.

- If slaves run away, they are hunted down.

- Then they are whipped and branded, and have their feet chopped off.

What was said in favour of slavery

Source B

The head of a state in the South said this in the 1830s.

- Black people were born to be slaves.

- God meant it to be like this.

- Black people are not as clever as white people. They need to be told what to do.

- Slaves are treated well by their masters.

- If slaves were freed, they would have nowhere to go.

- Slaves eat well and are cheerful.

- They know that their master will always care for them, even when they grow old.

- We need slaves to work on the cotton plantations.

- Without slaves we could not grow so much. We would make less money and be poorer.

Questions

1 Read **Slaves must be set free**.

Copy and complete this sentence.

People who wanted slavery stopped were called _____.

2 Read **Leaflets and speeches**.

What was the *Liberator*?

3 Read **Sojourner Truth**.

Who was Sojourner Truth?

Fighting quietly on the plantations

Slaves tried to fight for freedom.

Some slaves fought quietly on the plantations. They did this by working slowly. Sometimes they were clumsy. Sometimes they pretended to be sick. They broke the tools or let the animals out. In this way, they worked against slavery. But they did not fight openly.

Running away

Some slaves ran away. This was easier on the West Indian islands. Ex-slaves could live in the mountains or join bands of pirates.

Fighting openly

Sometimes slaves openly fought their owners. But they did not usually win. The white owners banded together to fight against the slaves.

White owners were frightened of slaves fighting to get their freedom. They treated slaves more harshly.

There are some stories of slaves who fought their owners on the next few pages.

Source A

A visitor to a plantation wrote this in 1793.

The slaves are well cared for.

I heard that they were graceful people, but they are very lazy and clumsy.

Question

How did the slaves fight quietly on the plantations?

Find at least two ways.

Slaves harvesting sugar cane in the West Indies in 1823.

Source B

San Domingo

San Domingo was an island in the West Indies.

The French part of San Domingo

Every year 40,000 slaves arrived in ships from Africa.

The white owners worked the slaves to death. It was cheaper to do this, and then buy new slaves from Africa, than it was to look after the slaves properly. French San Domingo had the highest death rate for slaves in all the Americas.

The French Revolution

In 1789 the French people fought against their king. They wanted freedom. The white slave owners in French San Domingo were very worried. They thought their slaves might fight for freedom too.

Boukman leads the slaves

In 1791 a voodoo priest called Boukman led the slaves against their white owners. Boukman and the slaves killed some of the white owners and burnt the plantations. The white owners asked the British for help. The British said yes. They wanted to take over the island themselves.

A new leader – Toussaint L'Ouverture

The slaves found a new leader. His name was Toussaint L'Ouverture. He was captured and died in prison. But the slaves won. They took over French San Domingo and called it Haiti. It was an independent country from 1804.

Source C

A picture made at the time showing the San Domingo slaves fighting their white owners.

Cinque fights for freedom

Cinque was the son of an African chief. In 1839 he was sold to two Spaniards. He and fifty other slaves were put on board a ship. They set off for South America.

The slaves take over the ship

That night the slaves fought the sailors. They took over the ship, and killed the captain and the cook. They put some of the crew in a boat and set it adrift. Then Cinque told the Spaniards to sail the ship to Africa.

Which way did the ship go?

But the Spaniards sailed the ship north to New York without Cinque knowing. Cinque and the other slaves were arrested. Lots of newspapers wrote about their story.

The first trial

The slaves were put on trial. The trial went on for a long time. But at last the jury let the slaves off. There was a lot of argument about it.

The case went to trial again – this time in the Supreme Court. This is the highest court of law in the United States.

The second trial

John Quincy Adams had been President of the United States. He was still a lawyer. He spoke in the Supreme Court on the side of the slaves. He spoke so well that the slaves were set free.

They went back to Africa, where they worked against slavery.

Source D

A picture of Cinque in 1840.

Runaway slaves

The free states in the North did not allow slavery.

Some slaves from the South ran away to the North. They hoped they were safe there. But they were not safe.

The law said that the slaves had to be sent back to their owners in the South.

Courts of law and black people

There were quite a few trials about slavery. Sometimes the slaves won. But often they did not. The case of Dred Scott was bad news for black slaves.

Dred Scott

Dred Scott and his wife and children moved around with their white owner. They spent four years living in free states (states with no slavery). Scott saved up to buy the family's freedom. But his owner said no.

Scott goes to law in 1847

Scott decided to use the money he had saved to go to the law courts. He argued that he had lived in free states, so he had to be free. At the first trial, the court said yes. But the white owner went to another court. That court said no.

Scott goes to the Supreme Court in 1857

Scott went to the Supreme Court. But it turned him down. The Supreme Court said:

Black people are inferior beings who have no rights which the white man is bound to respect.

So Scott and his family were still slaves. They were only set free later.

Why the Dred Scott case was so important

Before the case, it was not clear whether blacks had rights or not. Sometimes blacks did have rights. But here the Supreme Court of the United States said clearly that black people had no rights at all.

Source E

Questions

1 Who was Cinque?

2 What happened to Cinque in 1839?

3 What happened to Cinque and the slaves in the end?

4 Write down what the Supreme Court said in 1857 about the rights of black people.

Some runaway slaves joined Native American Indian tribes. The Native American Indians treated the black people as equals.

The underground railroad was a secret organisation. It helped 75,000 slaves to escape. Many stayed free. About 3,200 black people and white people worked to help the slaves escape.

Slaves tried to escape all the time. They had a much better chance if they had some help.

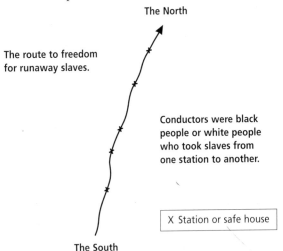

The North

The route to freedom for runaway slaves.

Conductors were black people or white people who took slaves from one station to another.

X Station or safe house

The South

HARRIET TUBMAN

Harriet Tubman was a runaway slave. She was a conductor on the underground railroad. She made about twenty trips. This was very dangerous.

In the American Civil War she worked for the North. She was a spy, a scout and a nurse.

After the war, she worked for women's rights and black rights.

She died in 1913.

John Jones was a brave man. If anyone had found out that he helped runaway slaves, he might have lost his job or even been sent to prison.

JOHN JONES

John Jones was a free black man.

John worked hard as a tailor. He became rich and was respected by both black and white people.

John and his wife hated slavery. Their home was a station on the underground railroad.

They also worked to change the laws for black people in the state of Illinois.

John had several government jobs. In 1874 he won the battle to open all Chicago schools to black and white pupils.

John Jones died in 1879.

Source A

Some slaves went to great lengths to get their freedom. Here is the story of one such slave.

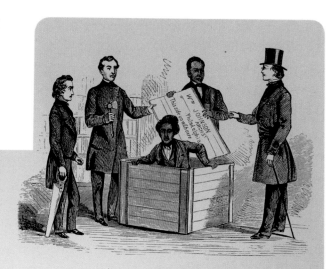

A drawing from the time, showing Henry Brown getting out of the box.

HENRY BROWN

This is a famous escape story.

Henry Brown was a slave. His owner would not buy Henry's wife. So Henry decided to escape.

I decided I would get in a box and be sent through the post to a free state. My friend, Dr Smith, said he would help me. We found someone I could be posted to in a free state.

I got a wooden box made. Then I asked for a few days' holiday so that I would not be missed straight away.

I got into the box with some water. I made a small breathing hole near my face. My friends nailed down the lid of the box and took me to the post office. There were labels on the box to show which way up the box should go.

I started my long journey north. At first they put the box head down, but luckily it fell over. Then it was put on the steamboat head down again. I was left like this for an hour and a half. My eyes were ready to burst from my sockets. The veins on my face swelled. But I made no noise. I was determined to be free or die. Then my box was turned on its side for someone to sit on.

At Washington I was tossed from the wagon. As the box fell, my neck gave a crack and I was knocked out.

I woke up as I was put on another wagon. I was head down again, but soon turned over.

I reached Philadelphia at 3 a.m. At 6 a.m. my box was collected and taken to the address.

People gathered round the box. One of them tapped on it. I said I was all right. They broke open the box and I was free.

Questions

1 What was the underground railroad?

2 What was a station?

3 What did a conductor do?

4 Who was Harriet Tubman?

5 What do you think would have been the hardest thing for Henry Brown during his journey?

In the 1930s, the American government collected the life-stories of people who had been slaves.

HENRY TRENTHAM

I was born on Dr Trentham's big plantation. There were about 400 slaves. The slave houses looked like a small town.

There were four overseers. They made us work from sun-up to sunset. Women had to keep up with the men. Most slaves cooked at their houses. We got weekly rations – pretty good, like what you'd have now.

We got a week's holiday over Christmas. We got our shoes for the year. On the Fourth of July, there was a big dinner.

There was a church where the preacher told us to do as we were told. We weren't allowed books, so I can't read or write.

There was a jail for punishment, but not much whipping. The Mistress didn't like the Master to beat us.

MATTIE CURTIS

I was born on a plantation, but me and my family were sold. We were sold on to a preacher. Even though he was a preacher, he hardly fed or clothed his twenty slaves and he whipped them bad.

My job was to mind the slaves' children while they were out in the tobacco fields.

The preacher never paid for us. So we were sold on to Missus Long in Franklin County.

Missus Long was a devil. I worked in her tobacco factory.

Then the Civil War started. She sold us on to someone who was just as bad, if not worse.

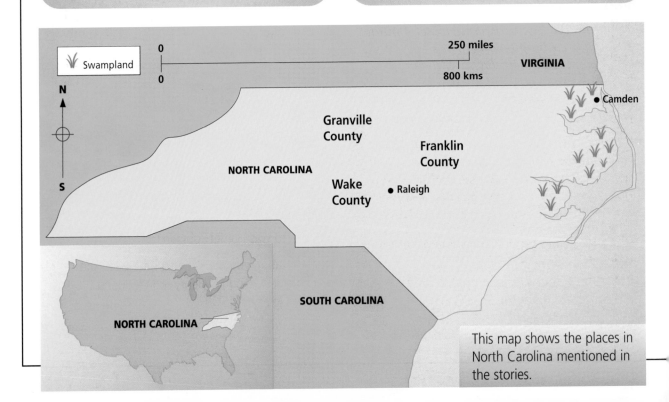

This map shows the places in North Carolina mentioned in the stories.

Source A

Five generations of slaves on a South Carolina plantation.

RIA SORRELL

I was born on the Sorrell plantation in Wake County. There were about twenty-five slaves. The Master wouldn't sell us and he didn't believe in whipping. But his wife was a devil. She loved to whip us when the Master was away.

Master Sorrell gave us good houses – two rooms with good beds and enough covers. We had a patch of ground to grow things on.

We had no overseers. The Master just told the oldest slave what he wanted doing.

We got holidays at Christmas, on Sundays and one day a month. He wouldn't allow reading or writing. But he let us go to church.

PATSY MITCHNER

I was born in Raleigh. My master was Alex Gorman, the newspaper man. But he wouldn't let us read or write.

They sold my mother, sister and brother to a slave trader.

Our clothes and sleeping places were bad. The food was real bad. The meat was all fat.

I never saw a slave sold in chains or a jail. I never saw a whipping – whippings were in the back shed.

Questions

1 How many slaves were there on Dr Trentham's plantation?

2 How many slaves were there on the Sorrell plantation?

3 What job did Mattie Curtis do when she was the preacher's slave?

4 Which slave do you think was the luckiest?

The United States

There were a lot of separate states in the USA. In many ways, they ran themselves like small, separate countries. But for big things like having an army or a navy, the states joined together. They made up the United States.

The southern states

In the southern states, slavery was legal. There were many slaves. This was because there were lots of big plantations, growing things like tobacco and cotton. Hundreds of slaves worked on the plantations. The southerners said they could not exist without slaves. They got more and more angry with the northerners, who wanted the South to free all its slaves.

The northern states

In the northern states, slavery was not legal. The northern states did not have big plantations. They did not need slaves. Over the years, they felt more and more strongly that the South should free its slaves.

John Brown

Feelings ran high in the 1850s. John Brown led an uprising of slaves in 1859. He was executed.

Abraham Lincoln elected President

In 1860 Abraham Lincoln was elected President of the United States. He wanted to free the slaves.

But more than anything, he wanted to keep the southern states and the northern states together. He could not do it.

Source A

Sam Houston was the Governor of Texas. He said Texas should not split from the North. It should stay in the Union.

After spending millions of dollars and hundreds of thousands of lives, you may win southern independence. But I doubt it.

The North is determined to keep the Union (United States).

The division of the United States.

The Confederate states
The Union states

UPPER CANADA

UNITED STATES

Atlantic Ocean

MEXICO   Gulf of Mexico

The split – the Confederate States of America

Six weeks after Lincoln was elected, several states left the United States. They set up on their own, and called themselves the Confederate States of America. Lincoln did not know how many more might leave the United States.

The Civil War, 1861–1865

In 1861 war broke out between the United States (the North) and the Confederate States (the South). Many black people rushed to fight for the North. But Lincoln said they could not be soldiers.

He was still hoping for peace with the southern states. He did not want to annoy them by allowing runaway slaves in his army.

But this did not work. There was no peace. The war was the worst that the United States ever fought. Hundreds of thousands of soldiers were killed on both sides.

Slaves set free

In 1863 Lincoln gave the order that all slaves were to be set free. Black people could now join the army.

Many black people fought for the North. But they were paid less money and fought in separate units. They often had white officers.

The end of the war, 1865

The war ended in 1865. The North won, so the slaves in the South were freed. Five days after the war ended, President Lincoln was shot dead.

Source B

A JOB FOR THE NEW CABINET MAKER.

A cartoon from the time. President Lincoln is trying to glue the Union back together.

Source C

An anti-slavery speaker urged black people to go to war.

Justice, humanity and good sense say that black men should join the army to defend their country.

Questions

1 Where was slavery legal?

2 Write down the names of the two sides in the Civil War.

3 Who became President of the United States in 1860?

4 Which side won the Civil War?

Black soldiers in the Civil War

There were many black slaves in the South. Some slave owners wanted them to fight in the Confederate Army (the South).

But the slaves knew that if they did, they would be fighting to keep slavery. Many black slaves ran away to join the Union Army (the North).

ROBERT HOUSTON

After the Yankees (the North) took Memphis, we were told to fight for the Confederate Army (the South). But we ran away.

Then we got taken on by the Union Navy. We got paid $60 a month for two months.

Then I got smallpox, so I was put off the ship on to an island. I cut and sold wood.

Later I was taken off the island and joined the Union Army.

I joined up willingly and have supported the Union all the time.

THE BATTLE OF PORT HUDSON

A white officer writes about his black soldiers.

My soldiers were mostly black slaves who had run away to join the Union Army. I had worries about their bravery. But I have no worries now.

They moved forward under deadly fire. When forced to retreat, they held together and split into groups to fight.

We held our position from 6 a.m. until noon. At 2 p.m. we were ordered to make two charges against enemy guns. The men did not swerve.

I have been in several battles, but never with soldiers of such coolness and daring.

The battle at Port Hudson, May 1863.

Source A

Families of black soldiers

The Union Army did not want the whole family. It just wanted the men. Some men left their families in the South. Other men took their families. The families often lived in camps.

Families of black soldiers.

MARTHA GLOVER

30 December 1863

My Dear Husband,

I received your kind letter and was pleased to hear from you.

It seems a long time since you left. I have had nothing but trouble since then. I told you how it would be if you went. They beat and insult me, and will not look after me and our children.

The children talk about you all the time. I do not know what will become of me, or them. Do not ask me to beg married men to join the army. I've seen too much trouble.

Farewell dear husband, from your wife,

Martha

Six weeks later, Martha and her three youngest children were sold.

JOSEPH MILLER'S FAMILY

My wife and children came with me when I joined the Union Army in 1864. My master said that if I joined up, he would not look after my family. So they came with me. They had a tent. Then in November my wife was told that they had to leave. My son was sick and they had no place to go.

In the morning, a guard ordered my family out. The weather was very cold. I told the guard that I was a Union soldier and that my son would die. But there was a wagon ready. The guard said they had to get in it, or he would shoot them. They were taken about six miles away.

When I found them that evening, they were cold and had not been fed all day. My boy was dead. But I had to leave them and go back to camp. The next night, I went and buried my own child.

Questions

1 Who were the Yankees – the North or the South?

2 If black slaves ran away to join the Union Army and left their families behind, what might happen?

The Civil War was over. The United States now made three new laws:

1 The Thirteenth Amendment abolished slavery.

2 The Fourteenth Amendment made black people full **citizens**. This meant that they were equal members of the country.

3 The Fifteenth Amendment gave black men equal voting rights with white men.

Did life get a lot better for black people?

Source A

Written by a black writer after the Civil War.

The South was a shambles.

- **Its big cities were gutted.**

- **Its farms were run down.**

- **Its banks were closed.**

About a third of its men had been killed or wounded in the war.

Steps forward

Freedom
Freed slaves could not have their families split up.

- Black people could live where they wanted to.

- They could also take the jobs they wanted.

- Black men could vote, sit on juries and become judges.

Schools
Free schools were set up to help freed slaves to learn to read and write.

Land
Sharecropping was brought in.

Black people farmed the land. Their wage was a share of the crop that they grew.

Black people could now help to make the laws, so that things could get better for them. Hiram Revels is taking up his job as a member of the Senate. The Senate helped to make the laws.

Source B

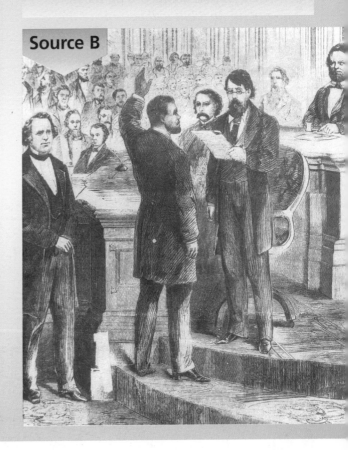

Steps back

Freedom

Black people in the South found a difference between their legal rights and what they were really allowed to do.

They had the right to vote, but some white people made sure they could not get to vote. They used threats and violence.

Schools

Many schools in the South closed. Some were burnt down.

Land

Sharecroppers had to buy their own tools and other things. Many found that they had to spend more than their share of the crop was worth.

'Jim Crow' laws

The southern states passed laws to keep black people down. These were called 'Jim Crow' laws.

Segregation

Segregation was one way of keeping black people down. Segregation meant separate places for black people and white people.

There were separate places on buses, in churches and in theatres. They had separate public toilets and water fountains.

Going back to Africa

Best for black people

Some black people and some white people thought it would be best for black people to return home to Africa.

Some land was bought in Africa. Some black people went back there. But it never really worked.

Most black people wanted to stay in the United States.

Question

Write out the three new laws after the Civil War – the Thirteenth, Fourteenth and Fifteenth Amendments.

Source C

THE KU KLUX KLAN

This was an extreme group of white people. They dressed up in white robes. They threatened and sometimes killed black people.

Many policemen and judges were members of the Klan. So they often got away with murder.

A Ku Klux Klan meeting.

What happened to the slaves after the war? Here are some of their stories.

PATSY MITCHNER

When I was about twelve, it was the war. The southern soldiers came through. They stole all they could. Everyone left the Gormans.

I went to Raleigh. I'll tell you, before two years had passed, two out of every three slaves wished they were back with their masters.

Slavery was better for some of us. Had no responsibility, just work, eat, sleep. Slaves prayed for freedom, got it and didn't know what to do with it. Slavery was a bad thing. But the freedom they got, with nothing to live on, that was bad, too.

I've been working for white folks (people), washing and cooking, ever since freedom came.

MATTIE CURTIS

Right after the war, northern preachers came around to marry all that wanted marrying. They married my mammy and pappy and tried to find their fourteen oldest children, who had been sold on. They only found three of them.

I married Josh Curtis and bought fifteen acres from the land corporation.

I cut the trees and sold the wood and ploughed and planted. Josh helped build the house, and worked on the land. I finally paid for the land, and had nineteen children. Josh and fifteen of the children died. I kept on going.

I'll never forget my first bale of cotton. I was really proud of that bale. I took it to market. White folks hated black folks then, especially if they were making something, so I didn't ask where the market was. I couldn't find it. I went back the next day and asked a policeman. He took me there.

Source A

HENRY TRENTHAM

After the war, I married Ella Davis. We had six boys and six girls. I think slavery was pretty rough and I'm glad it's all over.

Not all freed slaves became sharecroppers. Some worked for their old owners or did odd jobs.

A preacher visiting a free family in 1881. People could marry and know that their family would not be split up.

Source C

Not everyone wanted to tell their story. This is what Thomas Hall said.

When I think of slavery, it makes me mad.

I don't believe in giving you my story. With all the promises that have been made, the black man is still in a bad way in the United States, no matter what part he lives in.

No matter where you are from, I don't want you to write my story.

The white folks have been, are now and will always be against black folks.

RIA SORRELL

Our soldiers were running away. They took food, animals and even the quilts off the beds. Then the Yankee soldiers came and they took what was left.

When they told us we were free, we stayed with our Master. When the crop was in, the Master gave us part of all we made. We got some meat and crackers too from the Yankees.

After Master died, we moved. I was married by then to Buck Sorrell. We had six children – all but one died. We farmed with the white folks after that, till we got too old to work.

Question

Read about Patsy Mitchner.

What did she say was bad about the freedom slaves got?

By 1880 black people were supposed to have the same rights as white people. But in practice it was very different.

Black people went to their own schools. They lived in a separate part of town. They were much less likely to go to a good school, or to live in a nice part of town.

Say no to segregation?

It was 1898. A black man called Homer Plessy took a railway company to court. He said that they had no right to make him sit in a separate black people's carriage on the train. He said that the American Constitution did not say anything about this. But the Supreme Court (the highest law court in the United States) said that segregation was legal.

How could black people become better off?

The best way for black people to get on was to get a good education. But this was more difficult for black people than for white people. Black teachers were paid less money. Black schools had less equipment. Even so, some black people worked hard to become doctors, lawyers and teachers.

Source A

This college for black students was set up by an escaped slave.

Source B

In 1913, Woodrow Wilson was the first southern President since the Civil War. He was for segregation, and said this:

Slavery did more for black people in 250 years than African freedom has done in a long time. Segregation is not humiliating. It is a good thing.

Organise!

Churches were the first black organisations to help black people. From 1900, other people set up organisations to help black people fight for their rights.

Movement	Aims	Set up
National Negro Business League	To help black businesses	1900
Niagara Movement	To fight for black rights to the vote and equality	1905
National Association for the Advancement of Colored People (NAACP)	To fight for black rights	1909
National Urban League	To help black people who move to the cities to find homes and jobs and to register for government help	1911

These black officers are wearing medals given to them by the French for bravery.

The First World War

The First World War started in 1914. But the United States did not go into the war until 1917. Then many black people joined the army. They worked to get equal rights in the army.

What did the government do about black soldiers?

The government promised to train some black officers. By October 1917 more than 600 black officers had been trained. But they could only join black units.

Black soldiers could not join white units at all. Black men could not join the Marines or become officers in the navy.

War work

Garret A. Morgan, a black scientist, invented the gas mask. Many black people went to work in the factories making things like guns for the war. But white people were worried that black people would take their jobs. Sometimes there was violence.

After the war

Thousands of soldiers came home from the war. They were all looking for jobs. This meant there was more and more bad feeling between white people and black people.

The Ku Klux Klan started up again in the South. In 1919, there were twenty-five riots all over the United States about the colour of people's skin.

Questions

1 Look at the box headed **Organise!**

   a Which were the first black organisations to help black people?

   b What does NAACP stand for?

   c What was the aim of the NAACP?

   d When was the NAACP set up?

2 a What did Homer Plessy do?

   b What did the Supreme Court say?

3 How did black people help in the First World War?

4 Why was there more and more bad feeling between white people and black people after the war?

By the 1920s, black people seemed to be making progress in some ways. But in other ways they were not.

W.E.B. DU BOIS

W.E.B. Du Bois set up the National Negro (Black) Business League in 1900.

Du Bois was against Booker T. Washington's idea of teaching black people only practical things.

Du Bois said that this just made white people think that black people were not as clever as whites.

Du Bois was well educated himself. He became head of history and economics at Atlanta University.

Du Bois headed the Niagara Movement. This helped black people fight for their rights to have jobs, to worship and to vote. He was also one of the people who set up the NAACP.

BOOKER T. WASHINGTON

Booker T. Washington was an escaped slave. He set up a college in 1881. It was called the Tuskegee Institute. It was a segregated college and taught mainly practical things like cooking and woodwork.

Some people said this was no good. It just made it seem that black people couldn't do anything more clever.

Booker T. Washington said it was just as good to work with your hands as with your head.

He also said that white people needed time to get used to the idea of black people being good at things.

He was not against segregation.

Source A

The Ku Klux Klan attacked and sometimes hanged black people. A Niagara Movement meeting in 1906 said:

In the past year, the haters of black people have flourished. Step by step, the defenders of the rights of American citizens have retreated. We want to mix freely with whoever we want. We want the laws enforced against the rich, as well as the poor, white as well as black. We want our children educated.

Source B

Girls at Tuskegee learning how to be maids.

Harlem

Harlem is an area in New York. It was very famous in the 1920s and 1930s. There were theatres and lots of music of all kinds. Black people composed and performed serious music, musicals and jazz. They wrote books and poetry. White people and black people came to listen to Duke Ellington and Ella Fitzgerald. This showed that black people had real, original talent.

Living in Harlem

Black people felt at home in Harlem. Loften Mitchell grew up there. She said:

It was different from the rest of the city. It was like a small town. Everyone was welcomed and helped to find a home and a job. You might be cooking one thing when a neighbour would drop in with something else and so on, until a family meal turned into a party.

ELTON FAX

Elton Fax moved to Harlem in the 1930s.

I saw Harlem first in the 1930s.

Let me tell you one of the little things that meant so much.

Lacy, a big black policeman, was directing traffic. White folks had to stop and go when he told them. Where I came from, no black person was in charge in that way.

Outside Harlem

Carter Woodson went to Berea College, Kentucky – the only college in the United States that was open to black people as well as white. He set up the Association for the Study of Negro Life and History in 1915.

Dr Hale Williams was black. He was the first doctor to operate successfully on the human heart. By the 1930s, there were many black doctors, scientists and professors.

Questions

1 a Who was Booker T. Washington?
  b What did he do?

2 Why was W.E.B. Du Bois against the ideas of Booker T. Washington?

3 Write three sentences about what Elton Fax saw in Harlem that meant so much to him.

4 Make a list of the ways in which things had got better for black people by the 1930s.

5.3 BAD TIMES: THE DEPRESSION

Good times

After the First World War, there were good times. Businesses did well. There were plenty of jobs for everyone.

People thought the good times would last for ever. They spent lots of money and bought **shares** in businesses. Black people did well, though not as well as white people.

Bad times, 1929

All through the 1920s, people went on spending. Share prices went up. But then, in 1929, businesses started to do less well. This meant that share prices went down.

Some people lost all their money. Even banks lost all their money. Suddenly few people had any money, so hardly anyone was buying anything. Many people lost their jobs.

The drought

At the same time, there was a terrible **drought** in the Midwest of the United States. There was no rain. The fields dried out. Farmers lost all their money.

The Depression

The start of the bad times in 1929 and the drought caused what was known as the **Depression**. This went on for several years in the 1930s. As many as 50 million people, black and white, were out of work in the 1930s.

Black people lose their jobs

Before the Depression, there were some jobs that only black people would do. These were jobs like sweeping the streets. But in the Depression, white people were desperate to get any job. Often black people were sacked and their jobs given to white people.

Some families moved to find work. They were called **migrants** (see Source D).

What did the government do to help?

At first, the government did not help. Then, in 1932, President Roosevelt began to help people to find work and get enough to eat.

Source A

FATHER DIVINE

Father Divine was a black church leader. He set up shops to sell cheap food and coal to poor people.

He helped white people as well as black. He also set up restaurants, so that poor people could eat very cheaply or even free.

One of Father Divine's restaurants.

Problems between whites and blacks

Most people were suffering in the Depression. There were fewer jobs and lots of people had no money. White people hit out at black people. There were riots all over the country. In the South, hangings or **lynchings** of black people by white people were common.

JANE MAXWELL

Jane was born in the South in 1916. She began doing housework when she was twelve. She earned $1.50 a week. Then she got married and had a son. But her husband left. Jane worked while her mother looked after the baby. The whole family were often ill.

A friend found Jane work in New York. She worked as a live-in cleaner for $7 a week. She sent for her family. By 1940 she was out of work. But the government paid her $28. Out of this, she had to pay $22 in rent. But she was sure she was better off in New York, and it would be easier to find work there.

Source B

Black farmers talking about farming in the Depression.

If it wasn't the grubs eating the cotton plants, it was the drought. If it wasn't the drought, it was the rains.

What kills us is that we just can't make it here.

Source C

A black farmer from Mississippi (in the South) said it was not true that white people in the North were friendly to black people, while those in the South were not. It was not that simple.

There was a lot of hate in the 1930s. There were riots in the North. We had hate here, too – lynchings. But we went through a lot together. We were all suffering, black and white.

We weren't equal, no question. But we had white friends, white neighbours who'd talk to you, send over food, get you a doctor. I tried Chicago. It was worse up there. No one would even say hello.

Question

1 When did the Depression start?

2 How did the Depression affect black people?

Source D

Black migrant families in the 1920s.

The Depression was a bad time. It was a very bad time for relations between white people and black people.

Some black people began to wonder if it would be better for blacks and whites to live apart.

Go back to Africa?

Some black people wondered whether to go back to Africa. But they had been born in the United States. It was their home.

The Universal Negro Improvement Association (UNIA)

Marcus Garvey founded UNIA. He said:

- that black people should not try to fit into white society

- that black people should be proud of being black

- that black people should look on Africa as their home.

MARCUS GARVEY

Garvey came to the United States from Jamaica in 1916. He set up UNIA. Many people made fun of his ideas. But many ordinary people supported him and gave him money.

Garvey also set up the African Orthodox Church. In its churches, the pictures of God and the holy family showed them as black.

He also set up a shipping line to take black people back to Africa. But the ships were not fit to go to sea.

Garvey was arrested in 1923 and later sent back to Jamaica.

Source A

Marcus Garvey.

Source B

Some of the things Marcus Garvey said.

Black is beautiful.

Up, you mighty people, you can do what you set out to do!

Europe for the Europeans, Asia for the Asiatics and Africa for the Africans.

Question

Look at Source B. Write down the things that Marcus Garvey said.

The Second World War

In 1939 the Second World War broke out. The USA joined in the war in 1941. The war meant there was plenty of work:

1 The army, navy and air force all needed guns, ships and aeroplanes. So there was plenty of work in the factories.

2 The army, navy and air force needed plenty of men to fight.

Black soldiers, sailors and airmen?

Black organisations asked the government to train black soldiers in the same way as whites. They also asked for whites and blacks to work, nurse and fight in the same units.

The government said no

But the government did not think the time had come to treat black and white soldiers in the same way. So it said:

1 Black people could not join the Marines or the Air Corps.

2 Black people could only join the navy to be cooks or waiters, not to fight.

3 The Red Cross stored black people's blood separately from white people's blood.

Things began to change

One black soldier was promoted to be a brigadier-general. In 1941, the army began to train black and white soldiers together. In 1942, the navy and the Marines began to train black troops. The air force started to train black pilots, too.

Source C

Black women working on a train in 1940.

Equality

In 1945, black soldiers and white soldiers fought side by side in the same unit. By this time, over a million black people had joined the forces.

Wartime in the United States

There were plenty of jobs. Black and white people worked alongside each other. But often there were not enough places to live. Then white people could get angry. There were riots in several cities.

Question

1 Why do you think some black people would have liked what Marcus Garvey said?

2 When did black and white soldiers fight side by side in the same unit?

After the Civil War

Many black people moved from the South to the North. Many of them moved to Chicago. This was because it was easy to get to by railway.

Clarksdale, Mississippi

Clarksdale was a small town in Mississippi, in the South. It was surrounded by farmland.

After the Civil War, most of the freed slaves in Clarksdale became sharecroppers or small farmers.

The black people lived on the east side of the railway line. The white people lived on the west side. Black people crossed the line to the white side only if they were going to work for white people.

Chicago

Chicago was a big city in the North. Many black people went there, looking for work and more freedom. But black people were still not treated equally.

Black people lived on the south side of the city and were expected to stay there. They were paid lower wages than white people. They were charged higher rents.

Even so, many black people felt better off in Chicago.

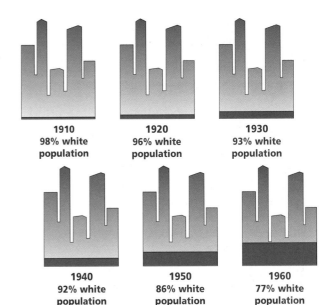

1910
98% white population

1920
96% white population

1930
93% white population

1940
92% white population

1950
86% white population

1960
77% white population

More and more black people moved to Chicago between 1910 and 1960.

Clarksdale

DON'T LOOK ME IN THE FACE

BE HARASSED BY THE POLICE ANYTIME

STAY SEGREGATED

ACCEPT LOWER WAGES AND HARDER WORK

LIVE IN THE WORST HOUSES

GET THE WORST EDUCATION

RISK LYNCHING IF YOU TALK TO A WHITE WOMAN

COOK THE FOOD BUT EAT ON THE STEPS

Chicago

ACCEPT LOWER WAGES AND HARDER WORK

STAY SEGREGATED (BUT WE DON'T CALL IT THAT!)

LIVE IN THE WORST HOUSES

GET THE WORST EDUCATION

How black people were expected to live in Clarksdale and Chicago.

RUBY DANIELS

Ruby was born in 1917. Her father was a sharecropper near Clarksdale.

Marriage

In 1934 Ruby married W.D. Daniels. Four years later, they moved into Clarksdale on a special scheme set up by the government to help people find work. (This was the time of the Depression).

Ruby's work

Ruby worked as a cook for $2.50 a week. If they needed more money, Ruby picked cotton.

In 1940 Ruby's aunt left her husband and moved to Chicago.

Joining the army

In 1941 Ruby's husband joined the army. Ruby found another man. She had two sons.

To Chicago

In 1946 she left the boys with relatives and went to live with her aunt in Chicago. They shared a small flat called a **kitchenette**. Ruby got a cleaning job and earned $40 a week.

In 1954 Ruby's aunt died.

A new man

Ruby started living with a man called Luther Haynes. They had two sons. But finding work was difficult.

Moving and working

They had to move to a flat in a poor part of Chicago. They had a daughter. So by now Ruby had quite a big family. She had a cleaning job and also got some money from the government.

In 1961 they started to buy a house. But Luther started to buy a car as well. They could not keep up the payments. The house went.

A new job and marriage

Then they moved into a tiny flat and started arguing. But things did get better. Luther got a job. They got married in 1962 and moved to a new flat.

A black mother in a Chicago kitchenette in the 1920s.

Source A

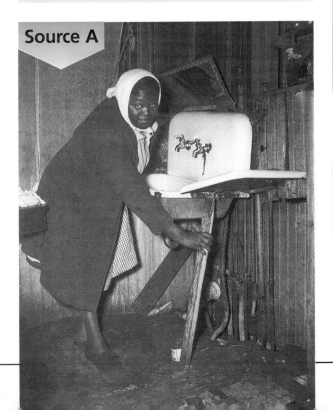

Questions

Look at **How black people were expected to live in Clarksdale and Chicago**.

1 Write down the rules that were the same for both places.

2 Which was the worst rule, do you think?

Civil rights

Civil rights are the rights of people to live equally and fairly. In the 1950s and 1960s, more and more black people worked to get civil rights for black people. Some white people joined in, too.

The right to go to a white school

In the South, black children were not allowed to go to white schools. In 1954, a case about this went to the Supreme Court. The Supreme Court said that segregation in schools was illegal. Black and white children were free to go to the same schools.

But some schools in the South ignored this. Often black parents had to go to court. They had to insist that their child should go to a white school. Sometimes that black child was the only one in a school of hundreds of white children.

Cafés and buses

All sorts of places were not open to black people. So they started to protest. They went to white-only cafés or sat on white-only buses.

Non-violence

Some white people in cafés and on buses behaved very badly towards the black people who were protesting. It was difficult for the black protesters not to hit back. But their leaders said that, if they did hit back, they could be thrown out of cafés, buses and other places. So white people got away with beating and threatening black people.

Boycotting

Another way of protesting was **boycotting**. This meant not buying from places that did not give equal rights to black people. There was a famous slogan: *Don't buy where you can't work.*

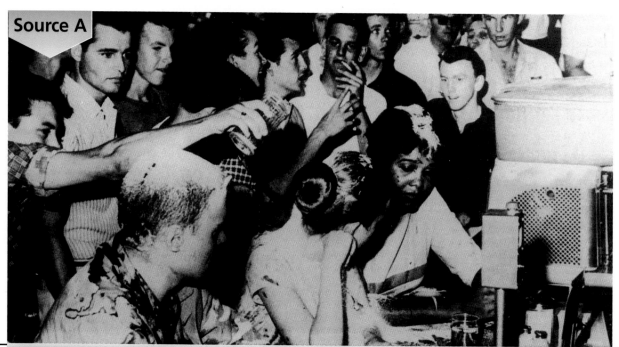

Source A

A black 'sit in' at a white café in Mississippi, 1963

The right to vote

Black people were given the right to vote in 1870.

But many white people in the South stopped black people from going to vote. This went on as late as the 1960s.

FANNIE LOU HAMER

Fannie Lou Hamer was a sharecropper in Mississippi. She decided to register to vote.

On 31 August 1962, I went to the county court house to register to vote.

What happened was that I got home and my children told me the plantation owner, Mr Marlowe, had been looking for me. He arrived soon after and said:

'Fanny Lou, you have been to the courthouse to register. We are not ready for this yet in Mississippi. Take the form back by tomorrow morning, or you will have to leave.'

I was fired that day and have not had a job since. People shot up the houses of black people nearby because of this. Two girls got shot.

Getting arrested

In 1963, I was on a bus when some of the others were arrested for trying to eat in a segregated café. I got out to help, so I was arrested too. They took us to jail. I could hear beating and screaming.

Fanny Lou beaten

Then they came for me. They took me to a cell. There were two black prisoners. They gave one of them a long heavy **blackjack**, *made me lie on the other bunk and had him beat me. Then they had the other beat me, while the first one sat on my feet.*

Becoming well known

Fanny Lou became well known. She later said:

If you don't lash back, you can find a real human being in a lot of people.

Questions

1 What are civil rights?

2 What did the Supreme Court say about schools in 1954?

3 a When were black people given the vote?
  b What did many people in the South do about black people voting?

4 Read about Fanny Lou Hamer.

  Why do you think the people whose houses were shot up did not go to the police?

Little Rock, Arkansas, 1957

Little Rock had de-segregated some libraries, parks and even the police force. Then it came to schools.

Nine black children were going to go to a white school. No one was prepared for the way the white people behaved. The white Governor of Arkansas sent in soldiers to keep the black children out. Thousands of people were horrified.

The President of the United States himself overruled the Governor of Arkansas. He said the black children must be allowed to go to the school. In the end, the children were taken into school by government soldiers. The soldiers escorted the black children round the school all day.

This worked while the soldiers were there. But when they left, the white teachers and white children picked on the black children. The nine black children knew that they must not hit back or they would be expelled. One of them was nearly blinded when a chemical was thrown at her.

ERNEST GREEN

I never expected it to be life threatening.

Most people didn't believe that the President would use force to get us into school.

When the troops went, all hell broke loose. They'd taunt you in the corridors, try to trip you, throw ink at you. There were water guns and you'd get phone calls at night, saying they'd have acid in the water guns.

They picked on the girls most. This bunch was really after Minnie. One was like a small dog, snapping at her all the time.

Then he touched Minnie's last nerve. Before I could say 'Minnie don't do it', she had dumped her bowl of chilli on his head. The school board expelled her. In school, they passed round printed cards saying: 'One down, eight to go.'

Some white kids tried to be friendly, but they really got it. We got through it with a combination of family support and helping each other.

ELIZABETH ECKFORD

Elizabeth went to school. Angry white parents shouted at her. Then an armed guard turned her away. She later said:

Lots of black kids were doing what we did. We couldn't fight back or we'd be expelled. That might mean the end of integration.

Integration means blacks and whites together.

The Children's Crusade, Birmingham, Alabama, 1963

Lots of people worked for civil rights in Birmingham. This work included a Children's Crusade. The black children marched towards the white part of town. They knew they would be arrested. In fact, so many children were arrested that the police ran out of police vans. By 4 p.m. nearly 1,000 children were in jail.

The next day, more children marched. The police brought in fire hoses and dogs. After three days, many people were in jail or hospital. Newspapers and television showed children as young as six being soaked with fire hoses and beaten. Thousands of people saw the pictures and they were horrified. Birmingham, Alabama, was shamed into de-segregating.

Source A

Two accounts of the Children's Crusade.

Audrey Hendricks: I was nine when I marched.

I was arrested.

They took me to a room where five or six white men questioned me. I was scared. I was only little. I was in jail for seven days.

Myrna Carter: On the Sunday march, they were waiting.

The firemen were there with hoses, and the police with dogs on leashes.

The police thought it was funny to let the dogs lunge at us, then pull back. We were scared, but we carried on. When the head of police ordered them to turn the fire hoses on, they didn't, even when he swore.

Source B

Marchers caught by a fire hose.

Questions

1 How many black children were going to go to the school in Little Rock?

2 What did the Governor of Arkansas do?

3 What did the President of the United States do?

4 What shamed Birmingham, Alabama, into de-segregating?

Thousands of people worked to make white people change the way they thought about black people. Here are some of them.

MARTIN LUTHER KING

Martin Luther King was a Baptist minister. He was also a civil rights leader. He made speeches. He got people organised.

Martin Luther King believed in non-violence. He said:

It is important to make changes in the hearts and minds of white people, not to break their bodies.

If you have weapons, take them home. 'He who lives by the sword will die by the sword.' Remember that is what Jesus said.

Martin Luther King won the Nobel Peace Prize in 1964. He was shot dead in 1968. There is now a public holiday in the United States in his honour.

Source A

Myrna Carter heard Martin Luther King speak.

At first, I thought I was going to be afraid, but the fear went.

Dr King's voice had a power like no one else's. He could somehow make you leap without realising that you were leaping.

Source B

The woman in the centre of the picture is Septima Clark. She taught thousands of black people to read and write, so that they could vote in elections.

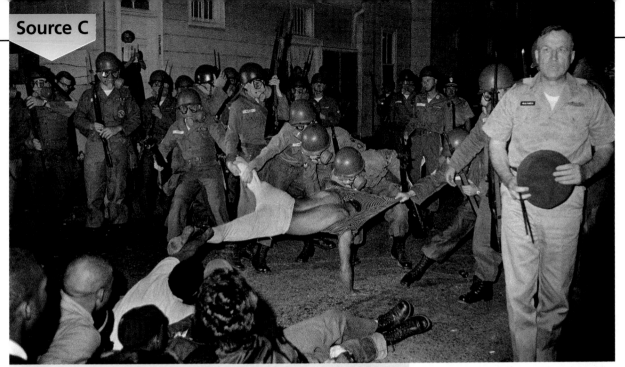

Government troops helped some black movements in the South. But they were not helping here.

ARLEN CARR

First day at school

When I started at Lanter High School, there were thirteen of us. We were all in separate classes. The head teacher opened the door and said to my teacher: 'He's in your class.' The kids saw me. You could have heard a pin drop.

Like a king

I'll never forget how you could be walking down the hall, and they'd just part. The first time, I was a little afraid, but then I felt like a king.

Some friends

After a while, their attitude was 'Well they're here, we've got to accept them.' We did make some friends, mostly from the air force base, where the kids had lived in different parts of the country. They'd been around black kids more.

The last year

In the last year, I asked a white friend to sign my year book. He wrote that he had hated black people. Now he realised that people were people, black and white.

Questions

1 Who was Martin Luther King?

2 Write down what Martin Luther King said about changing white people's hearts and minds.

3 What did Martin Luther King win in 1964?

4 What happened to him in 1968?

5 Look at Source B. How did Septima Clark change black people's lives?

6 Why did Arlen Carr find it easier to make friends with children from the air force base?

John F. Kennedy

In 1963, Martin Luther King led a huge march to Washington. The President was John F. Kennedy. He said:

The time has come for the nation to keep its promise. Those who do nothing are inviting shame as well as violence.

But little was done. Some black people began to think that non-violence was no use. They must fight back.

MALCOLM X

The X in Malcolm X's name stood for all the names taken from black slaves.

At school, he told his teacher he wanted to be a lawyer. His teacher said: *That's not a job for a nigger.* (He meant a black person.)

From then on, Malcolm said that education just made black people expect too little. He said that black people should be proud to be black. They should look after themselves.

Malcolm X was shot dead in 1965.

Source A

Malcolm X spoke to students in 1965.

How do you think I feel to have to tell you: 'My generation sat around like blocks of wood.'

What did we do? We did nothing.

Don't you make the same mistake. Don't try to be friends with somebody who's depriving you of your rights.

They're your enemies. Fight and you'll get your freedom.

Source B

Julius Lester wrote a book called *Look out Whitey! Black Power's Gonna Get Your Momma!* This summed up lots of white people's fears.

Malcolm X made black people aware and made them want to fight. He did not want to awaken the conscience of America about black rights.

He knew America had no conscience.

Source C

This was a peaceful march in 1965.

The march led to a new law. The law gave the government more power to force states to allow black people to vote.

This was a great victory.

But the next day, marchers in the same place were beaten up by police.

Source D

In 1966, these people lost their home and jobs in Alabama because they had registered to vote. Four days after the picture was taken, the pregnant woman started to have her baby. She was turned away from the white hospital. She bled to death before she reached another hospital.

Riots

It was one thing for the law or the President to say that black people had rights. But the policemen and soldiers who carried out the law were often against black people. Sometimes they beat black people up.

More and more black people became angry. They wanted to fight back.

Martin Luther King said:

Everyone underestimated the amount of rage that black people were feeling.

Things get worse

Black people started to use a new slogan: 'Black Power'.

When marches took place, there was more violence. The newspapers reported the black violence, but they ignored the white violence. Many white people read the newspapers. They were afraid of the black violence. They said that they had always thought black people were like that.

Source E

Martin Luther King said this to the newspapers and television in 1968.

If non-violent people like me don't say what you want, we don't get on the news. Who does? The extremists. By doing this you are showing extremist black leaders as civil rights leaders. And you're making violence the way to get publicity for our cause.

Questions

1 Who was John F. Kennedy?

2 Did John F. Kennedy support black rights?

3 Who was Malcolm X?

4 What did Malcolm X's teacher tell him about being a lawyer?

5 What happened to Malcolm X in 1965?

6 Look at Source D and read the caption.

   a Why did the people in the photograph lose their home and jobs in 1966?

   b What happened four days later?

   c Why did the hospital turn away the woman in the photograph when it could see she needed medical help?

Progress for black people

By the 1960s, many black people had got a good education. They had become lawyers, doctors, business people and mayors of towns. But there was still some way to go.

Riots

In the 1960s, there were many riots. Most of the riots were in big cities. Usually the riots were in the poor areas of big cities.

Why were there riots?

There were three main reasons for the riots:

1 Housing

Black people still lived in the worst housing and went to the worst schools.

2 Voting

Black people could vote by law. But often white people stopped them.

3 Jobs

Black people had the lowest-paid jobs.

Source A

Howard Morris, Director of the National Urban League, went to Newark in 1967.

I was visiting family and friends. About three police cars came round the corner. With no warning, they opened fire. They said there was someone with a gun on the roof. But they were firing at ground level.

My stepfather was killed. My brother was badly wounded.

No matter how well you do, there's still white prejudice. I had two degrees. I work with white people. But I was lumped in with rioters.

I was black.

Troops patrol the streets of Los Angeles after the riots of 1965.

Source B

Riots in Los Angeles, 1992.

From 1960 to 1992

In 1992, there were riots in Los Angeles and some other big cities. This was because black people still had the worst housing and schools.

Source D

A black woman spoke about the riots in Los Angeles in 1992.

It was pretty scary. All the burning, all the rage.

My kids are young. It was hard to explain why their neighbours were doing this. But then, it's been hard to explain why we have to live like this, too. Rubbish on the streets, homes and schools all beat up and not fixed.

Source E

Jean Carey Bond wrote this in the *New York Times* in 1994.

When my son was a teenager, he was walking home from school when a police car screeched to a halt in front of him.

Four white cops jumped out, guns drawn. They threw him up against a wall, patted him down and grilled him, a gun at his head.

A white classmate was passing and identified him to the cops. There had been a mugging. My son fitted the description of the mugger – meaning my son was black.

Source F

Written by the black politician Ron Brown in 1990.

In 1964 Fannie Lou Hamer fought to get just one seat at the Democratic National Convention. Now I am Chairman of the Party. We've come a long way.

But many blacks live in areas with:

- **poor schools**
- **high crime**
- **drug abuse**
- **too few jobs**
- **too little hope.**

A recent study shows that it will be seventy years before black men earn as much as white men in the same job.

Questions

1 Write down the three reasons for riots in the 1960s.

2 Read Source A.

   a Why did the police say they opened fire?

   b What was wrong with what they said?

3 Read Source F.

   What problems do black people still have?

Have things improved for black people in the United States? The last few pages have looked at the very real reasons that black people have to be angry. Here are some reasons to be glad.

Source A

John H. Johnson started his own business in 1942. He published magazines.

- **In 1942 I got a loan to start *Negro Digest*.**

- **In 1945 I started *Ebony*.**

- **In 1951 I started *Jet*.**

Then I started up black fashions and black cosmetics. Today I own the biggest black-based business in America.

Sport

Black sportsmen and women are at the top of many world sports. These include running, basketball, baseball and American football.

SPIKE LEE

Spike Lee is a writer and film maker. He makes films for black people. He said:

Film can influence the way millions of people think.

Source B

One of the most popular children's TV shows in the United States and Britain is *Sister, Sister*. It stars black twins.

Three ways to look at the history of black people in the Americas.

We've come a long way. Black people are not slaves. We have rights. We can vote, have an education. We have important jobs in all areas of life, from politics to the media. There are famous black American film stars, basketball players, writers, politicians.

We've had a huge struggle to get any rights at all over this time. And we've got far more rights on paper than in real life. We are most likely to live in slum housing, most likely to go to bad schools, less likely to be employed. We were struggling against racism and fear at the beginning. We're struggling against them now.

We are struggling. But we are getting places. History shows life in America hasn't been fair to black people. It isn't fair now. But it is a fact that we are not going to get equality easily, even though it is clearly right that we should. Maybe separation is the answer.

Question

Which of the three speakers above do you agree with most?

GLOSSARY

abolitionists people in the American South who wanted to put an end to slavery.

blackjack a short leather club with a heavy, leaded end.

boycotting refusing to get involved in doing certain things in order to make a point about something you disagree with.

citizens members of a city or country.

constitution a written list of rules setting out the ways in which a country should be governed.

Depression this happens when businesses collapse and millions of people lose their jobs.

drought this occurs when there is no rain for a long time and the soil dries up and plants die or cannot grow. This can cause a shortage of food and many people may starve to death.

independent a country or state that has its own government.

integration the mixing of people of different races (usually black and white) who had previously been segregated.

Islam the religion followed by Muslims that everyone should obey the will of God as set out in the Koran, the sacred book of Islam.

lynchings hanging people without giving them a trial, even though they might not have done anything wrong.

migrants people who move from one part of a country to settle in another part.

Muslims people who follow the religion of Islam.

plantation a farm or estate where cash crops such as cotton, sugar and tobacco are grown.

segregation the enforced separation of one group of people from another, particularly black people from white people.

sharecropping where a tenant farmer pays his rent by giving the landlord part of his crop instead of money.

shares a way of investing money in a company, so that you own part of that company.

slave a person owned by another person who is the master. The slave has to work for the master.

tribe a group of people who share the same race and culture.

INDEX